YOUR KNOWLEDGE HAS V.

Sören Weber

Data portability and relation management in social web applications

GRIN Publishing

Bibliographic information published by the German National Library:

The German National Library lists this publication in the National Bibliography; detailed bibliographic data are available on the Internet at http://dnb.dnb.de .

Imprint:

Copyright © 2008 GRIN Verlag GmbH
Print and binding: Books on Demand GmbH, Norderstedt Germany
ISBN: 978-3-640-22356-5

This book at GRIN:

http://www.grin.com/en/e-book/118916/data-portability-and-relation-management-in-social-web-applications

GRIN - Your knowledge has value

Since its foundation in 1998, GRIN has specialized in publishing academic texts by students, college teachers and other academics as e-book and printed book. The website www.grin.com is an ideal platform for presenting term papers, final papers, scientific essays, dissertations and specialist books.

Visit us on the internet:

http://www.grin.com/

http://www.facebook.com/grincom

http://www.twitter.com/grin_com

Data portability and relation management in

social web applications

Bachlor Thesis
Subject Digital Media (B.Sc.)
Faculty of Mathematics and Computer Science
University of Bremen

Submitted by: Sören Weber ▓▓▓▓▓

▓▓▓▓▓▓▓▓▓▓▓▓▓▓▓▓▓▓▓▓▓▓▓▓▓▓▓▓▓▓▓▓▓▓▓▓▓▓

July 28, 2008

Abstract in deutscher Sprache

Diese Bachelor-Arbeit beschäftigt sich mit der Synchronisierung von so genannten sozialen Netzwerken. Dieser Typus von Internet Applikation erfreut sich immer größerer Beliebtheit, was dazu führt, dass die Benutzer mehrere Identitäten, sowie eine Freundesliste pro Netzwerk zu verwalten haben. Daraus ist das Bestreben entstanden Daten portabel und damit wiederverwendbar zu machen, um z.B. nicht mehrmals eine Beziehung zu der gleichen Person zu bekunden.

Um dieses Ziel zu erreichen gibt es zahlreiche Projekte und Technologien, die bereits Teilfragen dieser Problematik lösen. Dabei gibt es noch offene konzeptionelle Fragen wie grundsätzlich mit diesem Problem umgegangen werden soll. Auch sind die Techniken teilweise nur für sehr spezielle Anwendungsfälle bzw. noch nicht für einen professionellen Einsatz geeignet.

In dieser Arbeit sollen die aktuellen Möglichkeiten genutzt und einige dieser Technologien verwendet und zu einem Gesamtsystem zusammengestzt werden. Dieses System besteht aus einem zentralen Identitätsanbieter, der als zentraler Speicherort für die Kontaktdaten fungiert. Über Schnittstellen können Kontaktdaten mit dem sozialen Netzwerk ausgetauscht werden wodurch sich das Beziehungsmanagement für die Benutzer verbessert.

Abstract

This Bachelor-Thesis deals with the synchronisation of social network services. This type of internet application enjoys great popularity which results in new challenges for identity and relation management. On one side the user has to manage different identities and on the other side a friendslist per social network service. From this efforts arose to make data portable and reusable for example in order to avoid re-declaring friends on every site.

To accomplish this goal numerous projects and technologies have been developed, which already provide partial solutions for this problem. The basic conceptual question however how to deal with the problem generally is still open. Moreover some of the techniques are only suitable for special use cases or else not ready for a professional use. In this thesis some of the existing standards shall be used to tie them together to one total system. This system consists out of a central identity provider, which functions as a central storage for the users contact data. By utilising interfaces this contact data can be exchanged with the social network service and by that improves the relation management for the users.

Contents

List of Figures

1 Introduction

Recent years have witnessed the great popularity of online social networking services, in which millions of members publicly articulate mutual "friendship" relations. Social network services have become a major application in the internet. Correspondingly the number of provider such social network services has multiplied and accommodates estimated 272 million users worldwide (Universalmccann, 2008). The mass adoption of social networking websites points to an evolution in human social interaction. These sites let the user create an identity namely their profile, which they fill with personal information. These identities can then be searched and relationships among the users can be made. A user can make friends virtually and by that creates his own social circle, that is why it can also be regarded as a reflection of the real world. Most of the users are part in more than one social network, which creates problems in terms of identity and relation management. At the moment there seems to be no consolidation among the services, but a further fragmentation and by that also a fragmentation of information.

In the real world people can be easily identified, but this is not possible in the internet as there is no physical contact. People using assumed names as an identifier which may be different on every platform. On top of this it is difficult to manage all the contacts which are spread over several services. At the moment the social network services do not offer ways to get the data out of their platforms to reuse it somewhere else. The use of separate networks may be wanted by the users regarding order and different roles they can slip into. In spite of these aspects there is an increasing demand for reusing and sharing the contact data to be able to manage the online 'friendships'. To overcome the disadvantages of fragmented data central storage has to be es-

1

tablished. In combination with exchange mechanisms it would make data reusable, which means all the social networks the user is part of could be synchronised. This is especially useful when entering a new network. It is like moving into a new city and already know some people.

Inevitable for such a scenario is that the information of the social networks are portable and that the user can be uniquely identified. There are efforts to achieve this goal, but up to now only partial problems have been solved. An overall concept seems not possible at the moment due to technical crudity and the difficulty to bring the different interests of users and social network services in line. Nevertheless there are existing standards that can be combined to one concept. This thesis will first analyse the needs and existing solutions in order to develop a prototype which is able to synchronise contacts in social networks.

2 Social network services

2.1 Definition

To outline the problem field first the term 'social network service' (in the following 'SNS') has to be defined. SNSs are a representative of social media, which arose from the Web 2.0 movement[1]. Social media means online applications, platforms and media which aim to facilitate interaction, collaboration and the sharing of content (Richter and Koch, 2007). SNSs can be defined with different viewpoints. "Social networks refers to systems, that allow members of a specific site to learn about other members' skills, talents, knowledge or preferences" (McKinsey, 2008). To be more general a social network is "an online location where a user can create a profile and build a personal network that connects him or her to other users" (Lenhart and Madden, 2007)

SNSs are based on interaction between the users which implies a web-based application as it is only applicable in an online environment and can differ in their services. They all have in common, that a user has to sign up for an account to be able to create a profile. Such a profile contains different information depending on the structure of the network, but in most cases at least basic personal data like name, address and birth date. In combination with a chosen nickname or an e-mail address the profile depicts the users identity in a SNS. These contents provided by the users are also called social objects. These objects plus the connections of the users among each other

---

[1]Definition of TechEncyclopedia (http://www.techweb.com/encyclopedia/): Web 2.0 is not a specific technology; rather, it refers to two major paradigm shifts. The one most often touted is "user-generated content," which relates more to individuals. The second, which is equally significant, but more related to business, is "thin client computing."

constitute a SNS (Wagner, 2007).

The goal of such a service is to let the users build and maintain their individual social network. Based on the 'population' of users different kinds of interaction are implemented. The most basic one is that people can make friends with each other and by that creating a contact list. This interconnection between user profiles creates a network which is called social network in this context. Usually profiles can be searched, so that it is easy to find people who already participate. In addition the inhibition level to confirm a friend request is quite low as the friendship is quickly established virtually and by that a user can build a wide network very fast. This of course highly depends on the number of users who are already there. The more people are member, the higher the motivation for potential users to actually sign up. Furthermore, with a large amount of members network effects become an interesting aspect of social networks.

This concept is the common basis of all SNSs and specific services are built on top of that. Further services are for example message exchange, virtual notice boards, photo exchange, discussion groups etc.. By this time there are hundreds of SNSs which differ from each other in the type of services and topic[2].

2.2 Present SNS usage

"Social media is a global phenomenon happening in all markets regardless of wider economic, social and cultural development. If you are online you are using social media" (Universalmccann, 2008). This statement points out the

---

[2]http://mashable.com/2007/10/23/social-networking-god/

2 SOCIAL NETWORK SERVICES

importance of social media which can be proved on the basis of the representative survey from Universalmccann (Universalmccann, 2008). According to that 82.9% of the internet users have watched videos online, 72.8% are reading blogs online and regarding SNS usage the survey reveals that 57% have joined a social network, making it the number one platform for creating and sharing content. Furthermore there is also a trend identifiable. Whereas in September 2006 only 27.3% of the worldwide internet users had a profile on a social network there are now over 57% using such services (Universalmccann, 2008). The growth rate is therewith by far the highest comparing to other categories of fields of application. In 2007 compete.com[3] determined that over 30% of the site views of the web are caused by SNSs with the major ones leading the way. The biggest social network MySpace[4] has now over 114 million users (Universalmccann, 2008), but the success is not only limited to one service. There are 16 other SNSs with over 15 million users plus many smaller ones (Universalmccann, 2008). There is also the phenomenon of niche social networks. In the face of the all encompassing large social networks a raft of more niche and sometimes exclusive networks are emerging (Universalmccann, 2008). These facts emphasise the need for data synchronisation. As a result of this survey it is stated that "Social networks are today the main platform for sharing content and have increasingly become the means to manage social relationships."

2.3 Relation and identity management in SNS

Due to the high popularity to manage social relationships with the help of SNSs there is a high demand to extend the possibilities to take advantage of

---

[3]web analytics company, available at: http://www.compete.com
[4]popular social networking website, available at: http://myspace.com

the data and the need for a new kind of relation management emerged. In the abstract SNSs provide on one side the functionality of identity management, so to express certain aspects of the own person. On the other side SNSs provide relation management, precisely managing and maintaining contacts (enhanced address book) (Breslin and Decker, 2007).

In the real world identity representatives or identity proxies (Becker, 2006) are used to identify people. This can be a passport, drivers license but also personal attributes like age and origin (Windley and Randal, 2005). There is however no physical contact in the virtual world, so that these different views on the identity do not exist in this context and other identity proxies are necessary. Usually a user of a SNS chooses an alias or nickname which is used as an identifier for this specific service. This however read little into the real person behind. In addition many users choose different nicknames which is also used to slip into various roles.

The relationships made on a social network can be viewed in terms of nodes and ties. The persons are the nodes and the ties can be viewed as social interactions or relations between the actors (Koch et al., 2007). That is why the unity of relations is also called social graph (Stöcker, 2007). As soon as someone is part in more than one social network, he is member of two different social circles. In network A he will have a different contact list than in network B. There will be differences, but also cut sets, which results in a duplication of the social graph. Using the platforms is therewith different to the real world where the user is central. SNSs however are not a group of people, but just a representation and the SNS just function as a tool (Vanasco, 2007). This leads to a confusing mix of diverse online contact points one can go to to communicate with his contacts. Of course it is still lucid in the case of two different networks, but the problem starts to get relevant for the use case that someone is in 3 or more networks. With each new membership the costs for coordination and maintenance of the networks increases. This would be obsolete if the internet users just do not want to attend more networks or just a few major SNSs will assert themselves and a allround service will come into being. But a closer look at the recent SNS usage reveals that there is a tendency to use several different SNSs at the same time. According to a survey of the research team cooperation systems in munich (Richter, 2008) 2,21 SNS memberships is the current average. Without claiming to be representative the survey indicates that there are a lot of users who would benefit from new ways to use the data.

Thus relation management becomes an important issue as the different social networks have to be reconciled somehow. In the original sense the social graph is portable and extensible in a flexible way (Großkopf, 2008). Following that to improve the practical effect of SNSs with regard to relation management the data has to become portable, which is embraced by the term 'social network portability'. But before thinking about possible solutions to bring all the networks together the actual need for it has to be worked out first. As SNSs are a quite new phenomenon and the market is changing very quickly it is not clear what problems simply need to be solved. In fact it may not be the desire of the users to bring all the networks together. For example someone is part in a business network and in a local party network. In this case he has probably good reasons to have separate groups of people being able to see the actual information in the different networks. The separation can also create a sort of order, because the user decides for one social circle

7

he wants to communicate with and do not have to bother about the rest which in fact shows similarities to the real world. As a social network is also attached to a type of service the user can keep up the separation of services, which is potentially much more usable than one allrounder service.

Consequently the fact that someone is in several different networks is not necessarily a problem, but a wanted structure. Nevertheless in case of similar SNSs the same information will be given more than once, like searching for and adding the same person to the actual contact list again in every network. Thus an improvement of this situation would be a way to reuse the information of the social network which is already available to avoid redundant user input and by that improving the usability. Portable data would also reduce so called lock-in effects. Network effects are a crucial factor of success, it means that the value of a SNS for a user increases with the number of total users and connections he has established (Schiff, 2007). To switch from one service to another goes therefore with high social costs (Westermayer, 2007) when the social network has to be build from scratch and thus the user is bind to his existing memberships (lock-in). In the end relation management can be brought down to simple human needs as Marc Canter (CEO of Broadband Mechanics) states "Users do care if for no other reason than they're lazy and they don't want to have to create all those relationships and upload their photos - all over again".

A second more important improvement would be that the user is the owner of the data. Actually it is his own personal information and his individual list of people he is connected to and according to "A Bill of Rights for Users of the Social Web" (Smarr et al., 2007) it should be a fundamental right of the user to own the data.

This also enables the user to manage all his contacts. The separation of social networks may be important for users in respect of the outer world, but on the other hand is to no avail for the user side. He obviously knows about his connections and therefore has the need to get a complete overview of his individual network which is spread over several SNSs.

Accordingly the goal to improve the identity and relation management in terms of SNSs is based on data portability. By getting the information out of the SNS the user can collect all this data which opens up possibilities to offer improved relation management.

2.4 Present data portability and its problems

2.4.1 Political situation

As already broached portable data is required to have a greater benefit of using SNSs. First of all however there are political issues affecting the access to the data. Besides small non-commercial SNSs the most important ones are companies who want to maximize their profits, so that they may have reasons to resist data portability. A crucial factor for such companies is the amount of users they have. Through that the platform increases in value, because the service is more attractive to users, as they find much more contacts and network effects get fortified. More users also means more traffic and this leads to better advertisement revenues (Olsen, 2006). The information the SNSs have about the users even allow for target-group-specific advertisement. The data is part of the business model. Big SNSs with millions of users and all their individual data hold out a huge treasure of personal data (Grob and Vossen, 2007) and it is even more valuable as it also includes the connections of people among each other. So these companies may refuse to

open up their platform, because they are interested in a proprietary access
to the monetisable data especially when the service is already very popular
and has reached the critical mass[5] of users. According to the survey about
the usage of social networks the most popular feature is messaging friends
(Universalmccann, 2008), so a SNS can also be regarded as an address book
and users visiting the site regularly to communicate with their contacts.
This could change and would reduce the traffic for the SNS, if the data is
available elsewhere also. Another disadvantage would be that competitors
could easily tout for the users when it is so easy to take along the contacts
from other services. Consequently at the moment such an initiative can only
be advanced from the bottom. Smaller SNSs working together to become a
strong counterpart to the big players that may force them to open up as well.

Besides these aspects data portability must also keep the balance of privacy
and usability. Privacy is just as important as openness and if it would become too easy to share data with external services security privacy issues
may occur. This is especially true for a central architecture when one identity provider stores all the information. In this case the identity provider
stores very valuable information. Moreover it can monitor the users activity,
because it is involved in every authentication process.

2.4.2 Technical situation

The current use of data portability concepts and the available technologies
is not prevalent. Most of the current SNSs originated as an independent
platform without an interface to the outside world. The most popular social

---

[5]Critical mass is a subjective measure of the point where enough of one's friends participate in a social network to make it valuable.

networks like MySpace and Facebook[6] are so called 'walled gardens', so do not offer possibilities to export or reuse the data available on their platform and the access to information is restricted to members. Thus the data is bound to the SNS and its proprietary formats. This is very different from the open nature of the web and leads to redundant storage of data.

In addition the user-authentication is decentralized and has to be done for each SNS itself. In contrast to that there is OpenID, a identity system that lets people use a single username and password to log in and authenticate themselves to OpenID-compliant websites. (OpenID-Foundation, 2008b). Although there are attempts to introduce this single sign on solution most of the SNSs have an own user account and authentication mechanism. This involves that the user has to to maintain his data on every platform separately. Furthermore separate profiles lead to the problem of finding contacts. The user have to do it again for each platform and as there is no general identifier like there would be in case of a single sign on mechanism it can be hard to find a contact. One and the same may have registered with different user names or e-mail addresses on each platform, so that a user might miss a relationship he would have liked to establish.

A decentralized approach to solve this problem is XFN (cf. 'Microformats'), which however is not widely used at the moment. The most important approach using this technique is Googles Social Graph (Google, b). Google provides an API to collect social network information from the web. Like the search engine is looking for words, the web is crawled for relationships. The API can be used to follow the links to friends, which in turn points to

---

[6]popular social networking website, available at http://facebook.com

other profiles of themselves and by that the user can discover an existing friend on a new platform. This concept however does not work out at the moment as there are not enough SNSs which save their data in the XFN-Format. Instead the "social network fatigue problem" or "social network update/maintenance problem"[7] is wide-spread, which means that people are tired of registering, re-enter their profile information and re-declaring their friends on every site (Oberkirch, 2007).

But there is a tendency to open up the services for reuse of the data. First of all RSS[8] has become a standard feature for the majority of SNSs. RSS is a standardized representation of information designed to syndicate information from different sources, which is mostly used for sources with frequently updated information. Facebook for example offers access to its data in form of RSS-Feeds. By that users can follow status updates of their friends, their news-feed etc. also on other places than Facebook.

Another way to open up the SNSs seems to be more important and more crucial for the success of the service at the moment namely providing an API. An API enables third party developers to reuse the data or even write applications that will run on the SNS platform. Regarding the reuse of data the website is not the only access of the service any more, for example one can use the service from a mobile or desktop application. Depending on the type of service this can become the preferred way of using it. For instance the content of the microblogging platform Twitter[9] is changing so fast, that it is not practical to check the website regularly. For this use case a desktop application which pulls the information from the service automatically

---

[7]http://microformats.org/wiki/social-network-portability
[8]a family of Web feed formats used to publish frequently updated content
[9]social networking and micro-blogging service, available at http://twitter.com

improves the usability a lot. Hence an API can make a service much more valuable.

The same is true of an API for applications that are embedded in the SNS platform. In 2007 Facebook was the first popular SNS introducing such an interface. Creating a 'social application' can be seen as a win-win situation. The SNS broadens the set of features it provides and the developer do not have to care of collecting enough users, because the application can access the already existing data of the SNS. In addition to the proprietary API of Facebook Google tries to establish an interface that can be used on more than one platform. Applications that implement the interface of Googles Open Social (Google, a) can be used on all the SNSs that support the API.

Moreover there are new services that make the data accessible from different places while the the the data remains on the servers of the SNSs. Following this principle the major social networks MySpace (DataAvailability) and Facebook (FacebookConnect) as well as Google (FriendConnect) have started their own data portability projects (Arrington, 2008). Another representative is Windows Live Contacts which offers the use of their contact data to other websites[10]. John Richards, Director of Windows Live Platform states: "we firmly believe that we are simply stewards of customers data and that customers should be able to choose how they control and share their data". But the user still has to rely on a proprietary technology controlled by a company and up to now all these approaches do not cover data portability in the sense that the user has full control over his social profiles, independent from a specific website. At the moment there is no possibility to export contact data from major SNSs to reuse it somewhere else.

---

[10]see Microsoft Developer Blog, available at http://dev.live.com/blogs/devlive/archive/2008/03/25/237.aspx

3   Current data portability solutions

Up to now the current needs for data portability have been described. There
are many projects that contribute to the data portability movement. In
addition there is the data portability group, "a grass-roots advocacy group
pushing the idea for users to be able to choose to share some of their data
between the services and being able to do so with peace of mind, security and
safety"[11]. It is an initiative to bring together and to develop further existing
techniques.

Regarding the basic architecture, there are two disparate principles to store
and read the portable data. One approach is to keep the data fragmented
and distributed among several networks, which means every time collected
data is needed it has to be gathered from all the sources. There is however
no additional party necessary. Contrary to that is the central storage of the
data on one server-system, which is synchronised regularly.

In the following the concepts and technologies contributing to the synchronisation of contacts are described. Each one is an approach to improve specific
aspects of the current state. This also includes the techniques used in the
concept of this thesis (OpenID + RDF).

3.1   Microformats

Microformats are a set of specifications that can be used to integrate meta
information into websites. The idea is to make the information also machine-
readable, which is the basis of the semantic web, "the extension of the current web in which information is given well-defined meaning, better enabling

---

[11]http://dataportability.org

14

computers and people to work in cooperation" (Berners-Lee et al., 2001). Microformats are "designed for humans first and machines second, microformats are a set of simple, open data formats built upon existing and widely adopted standards"[12]. The formats are quite pragmatic as they use existing HTML[13]-tags to structure and define the data. The set of formats can be used to make information of social network A readable and accessible for social network B and by that offer a solution for the problem of data exchange and synchronisation between web-applications. The data however must be accessible for the reading party. So microformats are extremely limited to the use case in which the data is visible and lives in an HTML page (Hammer-Lahav, 2008).

Regarding synchronisation of SNSs the most important formats of the Microformat-set are hCard and XFN. hCard is a copy of the vCard-standard[14] and represents people, companies, organisations, and places (Çelik and Suda). Technically hCard uses the HTML mark-up to put the information into the website. The formatted name is thereby required, the rest is optional. With the help of the 'class' attribute, which is part of the HTML4.01 specification[15], the properties are indicated, as it can be seen in the example below.

---

[12]http://microformats.org/
[13]Hypertext Markup Language
[14]vCard MIME Directory Profile, available at http://microformats.org/wiki/rfc-2426
[15]http://www.w3.org/TR/html401/struct/global.html

```
<div class="vcard">
 <span class="fn">Sören Weber</span>
 <div class="adr">
   <span class="type">Work</span>:
   <div class="street-address">Bibliotheksallee</div>
   <span class="locality">Bremen</span>,
   <span class="postal-code">28200</span>
   <div class="country-name">Germany</div>
 </div>
 <div class="tel">
   <span class="type">Work</span> +1-123-4567-8
 </div>
</div>
```

Figure 1: hCard example

The second important format is XFN (XHTML Friends Network)[16], which is designed for reflecting relationships between people. It uses hyperlinks[17] and the 'rel' attribute[18] that describes the relationship from the current document to the linked document. Attributes can be for example 'friend' or 'co-worker'. It can also take a value 'me', which means a link to another identity of the user in the web. By that a special hyperlink is created representing the relationship. The other person who is linked to can then link back and by that the connection is established. Thus a relation between two people is encoded between two hyperlinks.

By use of this linking the social graph can be expressed. This enables for example social network A to grab information about the users connections from social network B and may reuse it for its own service. But the information is limited to relations and it is not designated for additional information.

---

[16]http://microformats.org/wiki/XFN

[17]a link providing direct access from one marked place in a hypertext document to another

[18]http://www.w3.org/TR/WD-htmllink-970328#relrev

16

A general problem of such a decentralized solution is that all the information has to be collected from different sources to be complete. As so many parties are involved the risk is high that not all the information is accessible. At least it is a performance issue when requesting many services and processing the data. On the other hand the advantage is, that it can be used immediately, because no central party has to be established and it is based on the existing standard HTML and its hyperlink concept. This concept is already applied in Googles Social Graph project that provides methods to query aggregated social graph information from the web (Google, b).

3.2 XRDS-simple

Assumed information about a user is available in machine-readable formats (e.g. Microformats) on different SNSs. There is however no information available where and how to find all the relevant information of a user. Therefore a central catalogue which have this information available is needed. A suitable format for such a service catalogue is XRDS-simple. "XRDS-Simple provides a format and work flow for the discovery of resources meta data, and other linked resources" (Hammer-Lahav). So it is basically a discovery protocol for platforms who want to retrieve information. Thereby it provides information on how to find information about a resource and the format it is provided in as depicted in the example below (Hammer-Lahav, 2008).

17

```
<xrds xmlns="xri://$xrds">
    <xrd version ="2.0" xmlns="xri://$XRD*($v*2.0)" >
        <type>xri://$xrds*simple</type>
        <service>
            <type>http://specs.example.com/</type>
            <uri simple:httpmethod="GET">http://example.com/</uri>
            <localid>soerenw</localid>
        </service>
        <service>
            <type>http://specs.example2.com/</type>
            <uri simple:httpmethod="GET">http://example2.com</uri>
            <localid>weber.soeren</localid>
        </service>
    </xrd>
</xrds>
```

Figure 2: XRDS-simple example

3.3 OAuth

Microformats make data semantic respectively machine-readable. This concept however does not cover a security concept to share private resources. Lots of important information in SNSs are only accessible for users who are logged in and potentially for a specific group respectively just the user himself. In some social network platforms for instance a user can control what other people are allowed to see. If this is the case the data exchange only works if the inquiring party knows the user's credentials to get access to the data. Giving away the credentials is always a risk, one evil party could even lock the user out by changing the password. This problem is even more crucial when the user has to hand out his central identity provider credentials as the access is not limited to the one specific service. If sharing the credentials is no option it follows that the information have to be public to work with it. This however also leads to privacy problems, because personal information

18

and relationships are secured with intent.

A conceptual solution for this problem is to give access only to the information which is actually needed without giving away the credentials[19]. OAuth now tries to implement this concept as it is an open protocol to secure the API authentication in a standard method from applications. In the terminology of OAuth there is a service provider who holds the information which another service wants to access. This party who is asking for the protected resources is called consumer and first gets a request token from the service provider to obtain the users approval. If the user has logged in and granted the access an access token is sent to the consumer which then can be used to retrieve the protected data within its limitations[20].

3.4 RDF

As already stated microformats are a pragmatic approach to make data semantic. The Resource Description Framework (RDF) is a more substantial and powerful formal language for this purpose. The RDF-model is built out of RDF-triples with the three object types subject predicate and object. Compared to Microformats RDF needs additional RDF-mark-up, whereas with microformats one can embed meta data directly in HTML. Both do model user information and user-generated content in a machine-readable way. Microformats however were not intended to be infinitely extensible and a universal solution for the semantic web, whereas RDF has an open-ended design and the "ability to utilize, share, and extend any number of vocabularies" (Figley, 2007). This shows that RDF is more powerful and with

---

[19]http://oauth.net/about/
[20]http://oauth.net/core/1.0/

regard to extensibility the more suitable format to represent social network information which can be utilized for reusing information within Semantic Web compliant social media websites (Bojars et al., 2007).

One project who makes use of RDF is the FOAF-project[21]. FOAF stands for 'Friend Of A Friend' and is a way to describe people and relationships. It has been designed "to allow for integration of data across a variety of applications, web sites and services, and software systems" (Brickley and Miller). It can be used to manage contacts of social networks (Breslin and Decker, 2007) as it defines an ontology for representing people and the relationships they share. In FOAF Vocabulary each person is represented as a foaf:Person instance assigned with different properties (Bojars et al., 2007), like name, homepage, interests, unique identifier etc.. Worth mentioning is also the foaf:knows property which stands for a person known by the foaf:person and by that relationships can be indicated.

3.5 OpenID plus Attribute Exchange Extension

All the practices to make information semantic and machine-readable become usable for identity management in connection with properties that can uniquely identify a user. OpenID is such a protocol, it is an open, decentralized, free framework for user-centric digital identity[22]. OpenID provides a unique identifier and allows a central identity management. To identify at a relying party a Uniform Resource Identifier (URI)[23] is used for identification. The authentication is not part of the actual service application, but outsourced to the OpenID - Provider. There the user has to authenticate

---

[21]http://foaf-project.org/
[22]http://openid.net/what/
[23]a string to identify a resource in the internet

against, e.g. with a password and will then be redirected to the service site. Through this mechanism a user can log in with the same URI at every platform that supports OpenID. So basically this protocol solves the problem of multiple user logins and enables SNSs to provide single sign on. The standard is already used by industry giants like Microsoft and AOL.

OpenID can also be used for transmitting data to the relying party. In OpenID 1.1 there is the Simple Registration Extension (SREG)[24] to send basic data like name and e-mail address to the relying party. An OpenID Relying Party would send a request with an openid.sreg.required field and get back user information in openid.sreg.* fields from the OpenID Provider (OpenID-Foundation, 2008b). With this extension however it is not possible to define own attributes. Thus SREG is too limited to be suitable for a synchronisation of contacts between SNSs.

OpenID 2.0 however introduces a new service extension called Attribute Exchange (AX) which allows for defining additional attributes (OpenID-Foundation). Furthermore it is possible to store information retrieved from the relying party. As this exchange is part of the authentication process the user has full control of what will be sent to the relying party. To improve the usability identity providers let the user create predefined subsets of their identity data, called personas, e.g. 'business' or 'private'.

In general however the OpenID technology has very serious security issues (e.g. phising) which are not solved yet. This is one reason why it is not widely used. The problems of OpenID are not the focus of this Bachelor-Thesis, but the underlying principles which are very promising.

---

[24]http://openid.net/specs/openid-simple-registration-extension-1_1-01.html

4   Concept for a SNS metadirectory

4.1   Goals

Basically this concept meets two requirements. First it simplifies the login
process by reusing the login identifier and second it models the social graph
and store it in a central place in order to use it cross-platform. Analogous
to the needs described in section 'identity and relation management in SNS'
this approach wants to preserve the current SNS landscape and by that the
separation of the networks, as it is mostly wanted to have different social circles and application areas. The concept does however introduce a centralized
place to store all the network information and provide a complete catalogue
of the user's network. This comprises all the contacts having been synchronised with the SNS. This structure differs from the decentralised approaches
of creating a social graph out of all the sites by collecting the information
from different sites when inquired and make the user the actual owner of the
data.

As already stated the introduced techniques solve partial aspects of the current problems. This architecture is now the attempt to combine these solutions to one system. The practical use of the prototype may also indicate the
benefits of such a solution and by that contribute to the current discussion
of the data portability movement.

4.2   Concept description

This approach tries to solve the problem of synchronisation of contact data
in SNSs. Certain premises like the common use of OpenID are assumed to
build the prototype upon. These conditions are not given in the actual state

of the SNS. As already mentioned this is also due to the fact that the current standards are not sufficient respectively not secure enough for a commercial implementation. Further technical improvements have to be made to arrive in the real world.

The central element is the Identity Provider. It is based on the OpenID specification (cf. 'OpenID plus Attribute Exchange Extension'). While the primary advantage with OpenID is single sign on, the central identifier (OpenID-URI) has the advantage that even if the people use different aliases on various SNSs they can be identified across the distributed social networks (Bojars et al., 2007). The OpenID server is extended by the feature to store data about relations in the FOAF format. The essential part of the information is the identity URI, which can be stored as the foaf:openid property of a foaf:person (Brickley and Miller). As the OpenID specification does not cover the exchange of profile information (OpenID-Foundation, 2008b) FOAF is an ideal complement to hold the information. And with the help of OpenID Attribute Exchange (cf. 'OpenID plus Attribute Exchange Extension') this data can be submitted to the SNS. Collecting and hosting the user data are still part of SNSs in order to provide their services on top of it, as they do it today. The SNS has to use OpenID for the authentication, so the user can log in with its OpenID and get redirected to his Identity Provider. After authentication he can now decide which information is submitted to the SNS. When he decides to allow the submission of his contact data, the SNS then receives the information in form of a FOAF structured string as part of the response. This data can now be processed on the social network platform, which means a run-through the list of the Identity-URIs of all the user's friends in order to check who is also a member of this SNS. Each match can then be proposed as a potential friend for this platform. This is not only useful for the initial creation of the contact list, but also for regular updates and synchronisation. The data stored at the identity provider is therewith a metadirectory[25] of all the SNSs. As it can be seen in the figure the identity provider is involved in every operation.

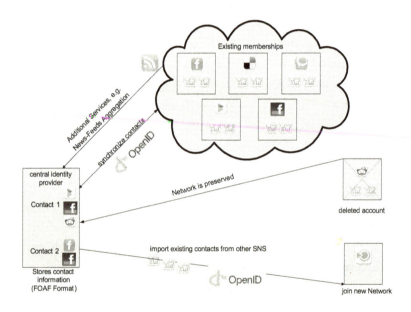

Figure 3: Concept overview

The result of this is that the user has his complete contact data at one central place. This characteristic of the concept provides new possibilities for

---

[25] A directory that contains information about other directories. It functions as a master directory gleaning information from all the other directories

applications. The data can be edited to function as an overview or address book. There is also the possibility to fetch information from the SNSs, e.g. all news-feeds, so the user can follow the activities at one central place instead of visiting all the individual sites. In addition network information is preserved even when a user leaves a network, because the information is stored at a place independent of the SNS.

5 Development of the prototype

This part is about the actual implementation of the concept. The functionality is based on a working OpenID Server and SNS.

5.1 Analysis

5.1.1 Functional and data description

The overall system function is the exchange of social network data between a SNS and an identity provider. The identity provider can send the data to a relying party (in this case the SNS), when it is requested. It is the central place where the user stores his social graph.

The SNS provides the function to send the most recent contact list back to the identity provider. Thus the data at the identity provider comprises all contacts that have been submitted from the SNSs the user is registered on with the according OpenID.

5.1.2 System architecture

The system architecture consists out of 2 or more subsystems. There is one central subsystem namely the identity provider, which is involved in every data exchange. The other subsystems are SNSs, which retrieve the data via an interface. For storing new information at the identity provider another interface can be utilised.

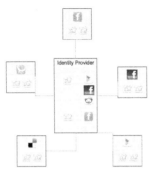

Figure 4: System Architecture

5.1.3 Interface description

The identity provider has an interface wherefrom the SNS can retrieve the data. It can only send the whole contact data it has from one identity, there is no partly transmission of the data. In addition the identity provider has an interface to store/update information about ones social graph, so that the SNS can send its contact data to the OpenID provider, which can then be added to the existing data.

Concerning the Human-Interface there is a dialogue for the user on the side of the identity provider to see what kind of information will be submitted. He can also deny the transmission of the data.
On the side of the SNS there is an interface to synchronise the contacts on the SNS with the information from the identity provider. After receiving and synchronising the contacts a list with friend proposals is generated, where the user can directly add people to the contact list of the SNS.

5.1.4 Usage scenario

This section provides usage scenarios for the software.

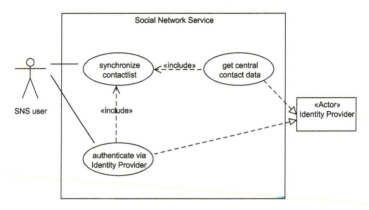

Figure 5: Use Case1 - Synchronise Contacts

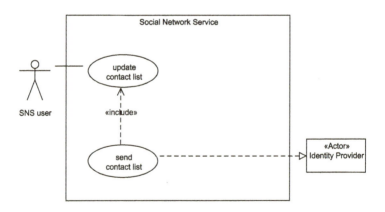

Figure 6: Use Case2 - Update Contacts

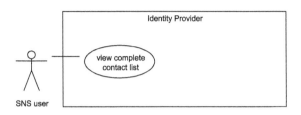

Figure 7: Use Case3 - View Contacts

5.1.5 Data model

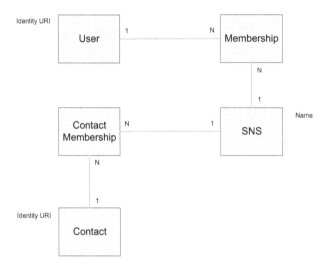

Figure 8: Entity Relationship Diagram

5.2 Design

5.2.1 Data design

The data at the identity provider is stored in the FOAF-Format. It is used, because it is an existing standard which meets the requirements. For this implementation only the unique identifier of the people has to be stored. The FOAF-Specification however comprises much more information and by that provides a good base to build extensions on top of. Following data structure depicts the structure of the FOAF-Format. It is compliant to the FOAF Vocabulary Specification 0.91 (Brickley and Miller)

```
<rdf:RDF
    xmlns:rdf="http://www.w3.org/1999/02/22-rdf-syntax-ns#"
    xmlns:rdfs="http://www.w3.org/2000/01/rdf-schema#"
    xmlns:foaf="http://xmlns.com/foaf/0.1/">
<foaf:Person>
  <foaf:name>Sören Weber</foaf:name>
  <foaf:openid>http://localhost:3001/soerenw</foaf:openid>
</foaf:Person>
</rdf:RDF>
```

Figure 9: FOAF format

The foaf:Person[26] class represents people and covers a lot of personal data types. In this case only the property foaf:openid is necessary. A foaf:openid is a property of a foaf:Agent which in turn is a superclass of foaf:Person. The property can be used as an identifier in the manner of the OpenID identity URI. On the side of the SNS the contact data may be stored in a proprietary format and it is function of the SNS to convert a user's contact list into the FOAF-Format so that it can transmit the required FOAF format to the

---

[26]see FOAF Vocabulary specification, available at http://xmlns.com/foaf/spec/

identity provider. Of course the SNS can store its own user data directly in the FOAF-Format as well, but most of the SNSs however have established their own database-driven format they want to preserve.

5.2.2 Architectural and component-level design

All subsystems are based on the open source Ruby on Rails Framework[27]. Rails is a full-stack framework for developing database-backed web applications according to the Model-View-Control pattern. It is used, because all subsystems are web-based applications and Ruby on Rails is optimized for these kind of applications and in addition can be easily extended (Thomas and Hansson, 2006). On top of that there is an OpenID server and a social network framework available based on Ruby on Rails. Thus the suitability and the existing solutions make it a good choice to implement the prototype.

Component OpenID - Server

Based on the OpenID 2.0 specification (OpenID-Foundation, 2008b) there is an OpenID Server in the ruby programming language[28] available. It is called masquerade and available under the MIT-license[29]. Up to now not the whole specification is implemented, but it covers the functionality which is needed for this field of application. The functionality again is based on a ruby-openid library[30] for verifying and serving OpenID identities. As the data structure equates to the RDF vocabulary, a RDF-Parser is needed to extract the information. There are several RDF libraries available for Ruby (Stadig, 2007). As for this application only basic RDF parsing is necessary

---

[27]official page available at http://www.rubyonrails.org/
[28]official page available at http://www.ruby-lang.org
[29]available at http://dennisbloete.de/projects/masquerade/
[30]official page available at http://openidenabled.com/ruby-openid/

the light-weight library Rena(Version 0.0.4)[31] is used.

Component Social Network Service

To implement the interaction between the identity provider and the SNS, a framework can be utilized. Lovedbyless[32] is one of the most active projects regarding open source social networks built with Ruby on Rails. It is a well established base to built features on top of. To enable the SNS-side with OpenID functionality again the Ruby library ruby-openid for verifying and serving OpenID identities is integrated as well as the RDF library Rena.

Both components are described in the following component diagram. Each component uses the interfaces the OpenID Attribute Exchange extension provides to exchange messages and data, in this case the social graph encoded in FOAF format.

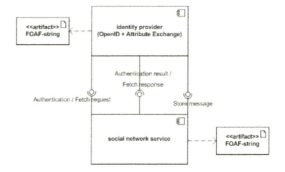

Figure 10: Component diagram

---

[31]documentation available at http://web.archive.org/web/20050208172416/http://www.fakeroot.net/sw intro/#id2480964

[32]official page available at http://lovdbyless.com/

The chronology is depicted in the sequence diagram. The fetch message is part of the authentication process, whereas the store message is a request that has to be triggered manually.

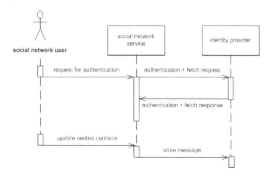

Figure 11: Sequence diagram

5.2.3 Interface description

The Interface of the identity provider is part of the authentication process and based on the Attribute Exchange Standard of OpenID 2.0. It consists out of the parts Fetch Request, Fetch Response and the Store message (OpenID-Foundation).

Fetch Request

On the side of the relying party (SNS) the required attributes have to be embedded into the request. The fetch request has the following parameter:

- openid.ax.mode

- openid.ax.type.<alias>

- openid.ax.required

- openid.ax.if_available

- openid.ax.count.<alias>

The value for ax.mode is set to "fetch_request". The ax.type specifies the type identifier URI of a requested attribute. This URI is used to define the attribute type. It must be an URI, but is free to allocate (OpenID-Foundation). There are however standard schemes (OpenID-Foundation, 2008a) one should stick with. At the moment however there are only basic schemes defined (OpenID-Foundation, 2008a), but in this case the identity provider is part of the implementation so any new schemes can be defined. So to save the the social graph the attribute type 'http://axschema.org/social_graph' is used. The parts ax.required and ax.if_available control which attributes are required respectively optional. The parameter ax.count determines the number of values for the specified attribute the Relying Party wishes to receive from the OpenID Provider.

Fetch Response

The Fetch Response message supplies the information requested in the fetch request to the relying party. Each attribute is supplied with the assigned alias prefixed by "openid.ax.value." as the lvalue and the attribute value as the rvalue. Attribute types are also returned in the "openid.ax.type.<alias>" parameters (OpenID-Foundation). The Response has the following structure:

- openid.ax.mode

- openid.ax.type.<alias>

- openid.ax.count.<alias>

- openid.ax.value.<alias>

- openid.ax.value.<alias>.<number>

The value for ax.mode is set to "fetch_response". The parts ax.type and ax.count are analogous to the request. The value parts assign a value to the attribute referred to as <alias>. If there is more than one value for an attribute type a number is suffixed. In this use case the value is a string structured in the FOAF-Format according to the data design.

Store Message

The opposite way is to send data from the relying party to the identity provider. For this case the OpenID Attribute Exchange Specification provides the store message format. The store message is used to submit personal identity information to the OpenID Provider; it provides the means for an relying party to transfer to the identity provider attributes that the user may consider useful, such as by providing them to other relying parties (OpenID-Foundation).

Analogous to the Fetch Response the identity provider expects the following structure:

- openid.ax.mode

- openid.ax.type.<alias>

- openid.ax.count.<alias>

- openid.ax.value.<alias>

- openid.ax.value.<alias>.<number>

The value in this case is also a string in the FOAF format as described in the Data design.

5.3 Implementation

5.3.1 Setting up the OpenID server and the SNS

Both components are built with Ruby on Rails and therefore an adequate environment has to be installed. The Rails framework is built with Ruby so first the Ruby language has to be installed. On top of that RubyGems the standard Ruby package manager is needed to finally install the framework as Rails itself is a standard ruby package[33]. Because Ruby is an interpreted language the applications are not compiled, so that only the source code has be put into the execution folder and one of the possible servers (WebBrick, Mongrel et al) has to be started. Furthermore each application needs a database. For the database server MySQL[34] is used and the databases are created according to the requirements.

To start with the data exchange the SNS first have to support OpenID. Therefore the login process respectively the authentication mechanism has to be adapted. The native mechanism is replaced and the SNS redirects to the OpenID Provider and analyse its response in order to login the user.

5.3.2 Attribute Exchange - Fetch Message

The basic authentication process can now be enriched with passing data using the Attribute Exchange Extension, which starts with the Fetch Request. According to the Design 'http://axschema.org/social_graph' is the attribute type for the social graph data.

---

[33]available at http://www.rubyonrails.org/down
[34]http://www.mysql.com/

```
new  OpenID::AX::FetchRequest
add  attribute  type  'http://axschema.org/social_graph '
send  request
```

Figure 12: Build Fetch Request (SNS)

The OpenID Server side does not have to be modified as the Attribute exchange is part of it. Merely the social graph data has to be stored for each persona. Therefore an additional database field is introduced which holds out a string in the required FOAF format (cf. Data description).

So the OpenID Server now sends back the authentication result and the Fetch Response including the requested attribute value. In this case the attribute with the URI 'http://axschema.org/social_graph' was requested and can now be read out of the response array.

```
IF  openid_authentication  is  valid  then
        login  user
        read  OpenID::AX::FetchResponse
        read  attribute  type  'http://axschema.org/social_graph '
        save  social_graph  data  in  session
        redirect  to  profile_url
ENDIF
```

Figure 13: Process Fetch Response (SNS)

5.3.3   Processing the FOAF data

After the completion of the data exchange the SNS has all the contact information of the logged in user to synchronise it with its own data. Therefore the received data has to be parsed in the first place. The information is available in a structured string according to the RDF/FOAF specification. During parsing the RDF a list of openid_urls is generated out of the embed-

37

ded information. This list is then used to verify if there are cut sets between the data from the identity provider and the SNS. This result set is then taken to show a list of the members the user is already befriended with on other platforms.

```
read social_graph_foaf out of session
parse social_graph_foaf
get openids out of parsed information

FOREACH openid from identity_provider
        IF openid exist here
                put to proposal_list
        ENDIF
END

show proposal_list
```

Figure 14: Process the FOAF-data (SNS)

5.3.4 Attribute Exchange Store Message

So far the data exchange from the identity provider to the SNS and the processing of the data on SNS side have been implemented. The store message now is part of the way back to the identity provider. Whereas the fetch request and response is an obligatory part of the authentication process the store message has to be triggered manually on the SNS side. It is implemented as an extra function at the profile page. So the synchronisation is controlled by the user. To send the information to the identity provider the data of the SNS first have to be transformed into the correct data structure. Hence a FOAF string has to be generated. Therefore also the RDF parser library is employed. To create the FOAF-File the user contacts are iterated and added to the RDF model object.

After completion the object data is then converted into a RDF String. This string is now ready to get transferred to the identity provider. The data exchange complies with the Attribute Exchange Store Message specification. The request is built with the help of the OpenID::AX::StoreRequest class of the ruby-openid library.

```
create new FOAF model sns_friends_foaf
FOREACH openid of a friend
        add openid to FOAF model
END
serialize FOAF model and save as sns_friends_foaf_string
new OpenID::AX::StoreRequest
add attribute type 'http://axschema.org/social_graph'
add value(sns_friends_foaf)
send request
```

Figure 15: Build Store Request (SNS)

If this data has arrived the identity provider it has in turn to parse the FOAF structured data and update its list of contact data. The list of contacts at the identity provider is already stored in the FOAF format and has to be loaded from the database. This FOAF String is then used to load the model. Through the extension with the RDF library the model object then provides the method add_property to add data. The data in turn comes out of the FOAF stream from the SNS.

39

```
read request
parse sns_friends_foaf_string
load social_graph_foaf from database

FOREACH openid from sns
        IF openid not exist in social_graph_foaf
                add_property openid to social_graph_foaf
        ENDIF
END

save social_graph_foaf back to database
```

Figure 16: Process Store Request (Identity Provider)

5.4 Appraisal of results

The concept is a solution to provide real data portability based on standards
that already exist today. OpenID however is not yet suitable for practical
use. But assumed such a centralistic identity provider would exist a complete confidence would be necessary. This however is not accomplished by
the OpenID specification, because it is not a trust system, but trust requires
identity first. First of all the identity provider is the authentication party for
all the SNSs the user participates in, so that the provider theoretically has
access to it. Secondly it can monitor the users level of usage for each SNS.
Thus to establish the centralistic approach it is crucial to induce confidence
in the identity provider.

Regarding the data exchange with the SNS another privacy issue remain
unsolved. To synchronise the contact list all the identity URIs from the
identity provider have to be transmitted plus the SNS knows which user
they belong to. By that the specific SNS receives information about all the

user's contacts on other platforms. A possible solution would be to split up the synchronisation into two parts, whereas the first part is checking which identity URIs are known at the SNS. This list then is used to execute the actual implementation. The SNS side however could still connect both parts to get the additional information. Further thoughts are necessary to cope with this privacy issue.

The practical use of the prototype indicates that the synchronisation improves the usability, because the user do not have for search for friends he already has declared on other platforms. Another benefit is the use of the central identity provider interface. There the user has a general view of all his connections. This prototype just provides a list with OpenIDs, but in combination with other information and the possibility to let the user also edit data, the identity provider could function as a central addressbook.

6 Summary and Outlook

The rapid growth of social network services led to a confusing market and the tendency of users to be part in several networks at the same time. This creates new needs in terms of identitiy and relation management. Each social network service membership can be regarded as one identity and for each of it a individual network exists. These separate identities and networks are suitable to slip into different roles and to subdivide the social graph into smaller social circles as it is in the real world. An approach to make data portable has to take this into account, which also has the advantage that the current established applications still can provide their services as they do it today. A new requirement however is to help the user to manage all his contacts, so that he has a complete overview and can share and synchronise this information with all the SNSs he is participating in. Thus the idea is to establish a central identity provider to share contact data between the SNSs. By that the data looses importance for the SNSs and the quality of service they provide would be the most important motive to use the SNSs which would be beneficial for all the users.

Accordingly data portability is a much discussed issue and a lot of projects attend to it. A bunch of techniques exist to make data semantic, to control the access, provide a single identiy and to represent social network data. There is however no overall concept yet, which is due to technical and political reasons. In this thesis a concept and a prototype to bind existing technologies together to one system have been developed. The implementation of the prototype has shown that that the existing standards in the data portability environment allow a synchronisation of contacts today. Using OpenID as basis for the central identity provider with the possibility to exchange data through Attribute Exchange plus the representation of social network data in the FOAF-format work well to synchronise contacts between SNSs. To arrive in the real world however further difficulties have to be surmounted. First of all the security concept of OpenID is not yet ready for a proper use with sensitive data. Second the major SNSs are not necessarily interested to make their data portable as they earn money with the users coming to their site regularly, because the data can only be accessed from there.

So in the future mature technologies and a new mindset of the operators are needed to propagate and realise portable data, but the history of the web has shown that open standards are beneficial for everyone. Starting from that many extensions and improvements of the developed prototype are conceivable. First of all the implementation of the interface can be simplified by providing generic FOAF-parsers that can be easily integrated in the social network applications. Second additional data like personal information to update the profile data or links to news feeds can be also centrally stored and exchanged with the SNSs, so the portable data goes beyond simple lists of friends. On the side of the identity provider the data can be edited in various ways for example the contact data could be analysed to show the social graph or the news-feeds aggregated to one master-feed.

Furthermore hybrid forms may come into being, so that the different approaches can benefit from each other as it is already done in a project with the aim to convert XFN information into RDF[35]. All in all it can be stated that the user benefits from the concept of a central identity provider as it is not the SNS but him who has full control over his social network data.

---

[35]http://microformats.org/wiki/xfn-to-foaf

References

Removing critical mass from the social networking equation. *The Blog of RealEstateVideo.net*, 2008.

M. Arrington. Data portability: It's the new walled garden. http://www.techcrunch.com/2008/05/16/data-portability-its-the-new-walled-garden/, 05 2008.

P. Becker. Identity substitutes, tokens and proxies. *ZDNET Blog*, 2006. URL `http://blogs.zdnet.com/digitalID/?p=63&tag=nl.e622`.

T. Berners-Lee, J. Hendler, and O. Lassila. *The Semantic Web*. Scientific American, 2001.

U. Bojars, A. Passant, J. G. Breslin, and S. Decker. Social network and data portability using semantic web technologies. *Science Foundation Ireland*, 2007.

J. Breslin and S. Decker. The future of social network on the internet - the need for semantics. *IEEE Internet Computing*, (6):68–90, 11 2007.

D. Brickley and L. Miller. Foaf specification. http://xmlns.com/foaf/spec/.

T. Çelik and B. Suda. h-card specification. http://microformats.org/wiki/hcard.

M. Figley. A comparative clarification: Microformats vs. rdf. *InfoQ*, 2007.

Google. Google open social. http://code.google.com/apis/opensocial, a.

Google. Google social graph. http://code.google.com/apis/socialgraph/, b.

H. L. Grob and G. Vossen. Entwicklungen im web 2.0 aus technischer, ökonomischer und sozialer sicht., 2007.

P. Großkopf. Anforderungen und Chancen von Social Network Portability. Diplomarbeit, Westfälische Wilhelms-Universität Münster, 2008.

E. Hammer-Lahav. Putting xrds-simple in context. *hueniverse Blog*, 2008.

E. Hammer-Lahav. Xrds-simple specification. http://xrds-simple.net/core/1.0/.

M. Koch, Richter, Alexander, and A. Schlosser. Produkte zum it-gestützten social networking in unternehmen. In *Wirtschaftsinformatik*, pages 448–455. 2007.

A. Lenhart and M. Madden. Social networking websites and teens. http://www.pewinternet.org/pdfs/PIP_SNS_Data_Memo_Jan_2007.pdf, Januar 2007.

McKinsey. How businesses are using web 2.0. http://www.mckinseyquarterly.com/How_businesses_are_using_Web_20_A_McKinsey_Global_Survey_1913_ 07 2008.

B. Oberkirch. Designing portable social networks. *Like It Matters Blog*, 2007. URL `http://www.brianoberkirch.com/2007/08/02/designing-portable-social-networks/`.

S. Olsen. Turning social network traffic into dollars. *ZDNET*, 2006. URL
`http://news.zdnet.com/2100-9588_22-149941.html`.

OpenID-Foundation. Openid attribute exchange specification.
http://openid.net/specs/openid-attribute-exchange-1_0-05.html/.

OpenID-Foundation. Ax-schema types. http://www.axschema.org/types/, 2008a.

OpenID-Foundation. Openid specification.
http://openid.net/specs/openid-authentication-2_0.html, 2008b.

A. Richter. Erste ergebnisse der umfrage zur privaten nutzung von
social-networking-services (sns) in deutschland.
http://www.cnss.de/files/sns-umfrage_final1.pdf, 2008.

A. Richter and M. Koch. *Social Software - Status Quo und Zukunft*. Universität der
Bundeswehr München, 2007.

A. Schiff. Social network portability. *26econ Blog*, 2007. URL
`http://www.26econ.com/social-network-portability/`.

J. Smarr, M. Canter, R. Scoble, and M. Arrington. A bill of rights for users of the social
web. *Open Social Web*, 2007. URL
`http://opensocialweb.org/2007/09/05/bill-of-rights/`.

P. Stadig. The state of rdf support in ruby.
http://paul.stadig.name/2007/10/26/the-state-of-rdf-support-in-ruby-2007, 2007.

C. Stöcker. It-giganten stricken am menschen-netz. *Spiegel Online*, 2007. URL
`http://www.spiegel.de/netzwelt/web/0,1518,507689,00.html`.

D. Thomas and D. H. Hansson. *Agile Web Development with Rails*. Pragmatic
Bookshelf, 2006.

Universalmccann. Social media tracker wave 3 survey about the impact of social media.
http://www.universalmccann.com/Assets/2413%20-
%20Wave%203%3complete%20document%20AW%203_20080418124523.pdf, 04
2008.

J. Vanasco. Online identities and social mapping: Iii. an analysis of social network
portability. In *Identity Research*. 2007.

O. Wagner. Portable social networks meetup. *Agenturblog*, 2007. URL
`http://www.agenturblog.de/2007-10/portable-social-networks-meetup/`.

T. Westermayer. Wechsel nicht möglich. *Telepolis Blog*, 2007. URL
`http://www.heise.de/tp/r4/artikel/25/25536/1.html`.

P. J. Windley and A. Randal. *Digital Identity*, volume 1. Tatiana Apandi, 2005.

A Appendix

A.1   Source code digest

```
openid = params [: openid_identifier ]
oidreq = consumer . begin (openid )

#build Fetch Request for Attribute Exchange
axreq = OpenID :: AX :: FetchRequest . new
axreq . add ( OpenID :: AX :: AttrInfo . new
( 'http://axschema. org / social_graph ', 'social_graph ', true ))

#send request
redirect_to oidreq . redirect_url ( home_url , openid_complete_url )
```

Figure 17: Build Fetch Request

```
oidresp = consumer . complete (parameters , openid_complete_url )
openid = oidresp . display_identifier
  if OpenID :: Consumer :: SUCCESS
    user_data = {}
    user_data [: openid_url ] = openid
    if axresp = OpenID :: AX :: FetchResponse . from_success_response ( oidresp )
      @user = User . login_with_openid ( user_data )
      session [: social_graph ] = axresp . data [ 'http://axschema. org / social_graph '] [0]
      redirect_to profile_url ( @user . profile )
    end
  end
```

Figure 18: Process Fetch Response

```
#load FOAF-data
model = Rena :: MemModel . new
model . load ( @social_graph , : content_type  => 'application / rdf+xml ')

#Parse it
friends = Array . new
model . each_resource { | res |
      friends << res . get_property (" http://xmlns.com/foaf /0.1/ openid "). to_s
}

#check for matches
openid_urls = friends . join ( '",'",' ')
friends_here = User . find (: all ,
                    : conditions  => [ 'openid_url IN (?) ', openid_urls ])
@profiles_here = Array . new
friends_here . each { | friend |
      @profiles_here << friend . profile
}
```

Figure 19: Parsing the RDF-File

46

```
model = Rena::MemModel.new
res = model.create_resource
@user.friends.each { | friend |
        blank = model.create_resource
        blank.add_property( RDF::Type,
                model.create_resource("http://xmlns.com/foaf/0.1/Person") )
        blank.add_property("http://xmlns.com/foaf/0.1/openid",
                Rena::PlainLiteral.new(friend.openid_url))
}
model.save( @foaf_string, :content_type => "application/rdf+xml")
```

Figure 20: Generate the FOAF-File

```
#build Store Request for Attribute Exchange
axstrreq = OpenID::AX::StoreRequest.new
axstrreq.add_value(http://axschema.org/social_graph, @foaf_string)
```

Figure 21: Build Store Request

```
#Data from SNS
model = Rena::MemModel.new
model.load( @social_graph, :content_type  => 'application/rdf+xml' )

friends_from_sns = Array.new
model.each_resource { | res |
      friends_from_sns << res.get_property
                ("http://xmlns.com/foaf/0.1/openid").to_s
}

#Data at Identity Provider
@persona = current_account.persona.find(:first)
model = Rena::MemModel.new
model.load( @persona.social_graph, :content_type  => 'application/rdf+xml' )

friends_IP = Array.new
model.each_resource { | res |
      friends_IP << res.get_property
                ("http://xmlns.com/foaf/0.1/openid").to_s
}
#merge data
friends_all = Array.new
friends_all = friends_from_sns | friends_IP
friends_all.uniq!

#create RDF model
model = Rena::MemModel.new
# create the resource
res = model.create_resource
friends_all.each { | friend |
      blank = model.create_resource
      blank.add_property( RDF::Type,
                model.create_resource("http://xmlns.com/foaf/0.1/Person") )
      blank.add_property("http://xmlns.com/foaf/0.1/openid",
                Rena::PlainLiteral.new(friend))
}

model.save( @persona.social_graph, :content_type  => "application/rdf+xml")
```

Figure 22: Update information at Identity Provicer